BEING HUMAN AFTER 1492

BEING HUMAN AFTER 1492

Richard Pithouse

DARAJA PRESS

Published by Daraja Press
https://darajapress.com

This essay was first published by The Con, Johannesburg on November 16, 2016

Cover design: Kate McDonnell
Cover image: Anastasya Eliseeva

Library and Archives Canada Cataloguing in Publication
Title: Being human after 1492 / Richard Pithouse.
Names: Pithouse, Richard, 1970- author.
Description: Series statement: Thinking freedom
Identifiers: Canadiana (print) 20200397907 | Canadiana (ebook) 20200398474 | ISBN 9781988832852 (softcover) | ISBN 9781988832869 (PDF)
Subjects: LCSH: Racism—History. | LCSH: World history.
Classification: LCC HT1507 .P58 2020 | DDC 305.8009—dc23

Contents

Prelude   1

The Christian Ideology   2

The First Emergence of the Racial Ideology   5

1492   7

The English in the New World   13

The Tempest   16

The European Ideology   18

The Many-Headed Hydra   20

The Radical Enlightenment   22

Liberalism   24

Capitalism   28

Revolution and Racist Rationality   31

A Counter-Humanism?   34

About the author   37

Prelude

On 2 January 1492, Muhammad XII of Granada conceded defeat to Isabella and Ferdinand, the Catholic monarchs of Castile and Aragon. His surrender came after ten years of war and marked the end of almost eight centuries of Islamic power in the Iberian Peninsular. The Ottoman Empire was a powerful presence in the East – from what is now Serbia to Greece and on to the lands north of the Black Sea, now part of Ukraine.

Isabella and Ferdinand had been running the Inquisition – a campaign of terror primarily aimed at forcing Jewish and Muslim converts to Christianity to conform to orthodoxy – since 1478. Christian persecution of Jews in Spain had a long history, reaching back to the Synod of Elvira in the first years of the fourth century, and included the notorious massacre that followed an inflammatory sermon by a demagogic cleric on Ash Wednesday in 1391. Muslim rule had provided a long respite, during which there was significant Jewish flourishing. But after the defeat of Muhammad XII, Isabella and Ferdinand moved swiftly to secure the ideological base for their authority, and to expropriate wealth. On 31 March, an edict was issued expelling practicing Jews from Spain. Many found sanctuary in North Africa and the Ottoman Empire.

The Christian Ideology

Christianity arrived in Europe from what is now the Middle East. Following his conversion outside Damascus Paul the Apostle, born in Tarsus near the Mediterranean coast of what is now Turkey, turned a small apocalyptic Jewish sect, founded in Palestine, into a new religion with a universal address.

Two letters by Paul, both probably written in Ephesus, also on the Mediterranean coast of what is now Turkey, are often taken to be significant moments in the development of the new religion. In his Epistle to the Galatians Paul insisted that: "There is neither Jew nor Greek, there is neither slave nor free man, there is neither male nor female". In the first Epistle to the Corinthians, he declared that: "Circumcision is nothing and uncircumcision is nothing."

Christianity quickly spread through the Roman Empire, and beyond to Ethiopia, Persia and India. It sustained Paul's universal address – anybody could convert and be reborn as a Christian – but assumed that only its followers had obtained the full humanity offered by divine revelation. It was particularly attractive to oppressed groups in the Roman Empire, including slaves. The first state to adopt the new religion was the Kingdom of Armenia in 301. In 313, Constantine, the Roman Emperor, issued an edict in

Milan that granted religious freedom to Christians. In 380, Christianity became the state religion of the Roman Empire. It's greatest intellectual was Augustine of Hippo, a convert from what is now Souk Ahras in Algeria. Much of Europe was still pagan, and would remain so for centuries, particularly towards the North and the East.

Augustine took the view that slavery was both inevitable and consequent to sin. The Christian Church did not oppose slavery but from 538 it began to insist that Jews and pagans be prevented from owning Christian slaves. Pope Gregory I, who held the Papacy from 590 to 604, took an obsessive interest in preventing Jews from owning Christian slaves.

Another new religion with a universal address, Islam, rushed out of Arabia in the seventh century. Its armies quickly defeated the Persian Empire and parts of Byzantium, the last remnant of the Roman Empire. Spain was invaded in 771. The advance into Europe was stopped near Tours, in modern France, in 732. Kwame Appiah writes that a Latin account of the battle, written in Spain in 754, marks the first use of the term Europe – previously a solely geographic signifier – to refer to a people.

The roots of the emergence of Europe as a political project on an international stage are often traced back to 27 November 1095. This is when Pope Urban II gave the speech, in the French city of Claremont, that authorised the First Crusade. The soldiers who would soon leave for Constantinople, and then continue on to Jerusalem, were offered divine forgiveness in advance for the sins to be committed against the enemy in the East. The Pope also issued a bull that introduced the idea of Terra Nullius (Empty Land). It meant that lands held by people who were not Christian could be expropriated. The profession of faith had become a universal vector of exclusion from the count of the fully human.

In 1096, the fervour aroused by the Crusade resulted in pogroms against Jews in parts of what are now France and Germany. Muslims and Jews were later massacred in Jerusalem when the city fell to the Crusaders in 1099. The Crusades to the East continued for almost two hundred years. There were also military campaigns against pagans, followed by forced conversions, in the North and East of Europe. The Fourth Crusade ended in the sacking of Constantinople in 1204. Most of its great library was destroyed but a few manuscripts – including philosophy from Ancient Greece – were returned to Europe. Along with manuscripts attained from Muslim scholars in Spain and Sicily, and translated from Arabic, they became the foundation of the secular intellectual resources that would be central to the development of the first universities in Italy, France and England, and the European Renaissance that began in the 14th Century.

The First Emergence of the Racial Ideology

In the fifteenth century, Mediterranean trade reached out to China, the Levant and India. Slaves were central to that trade. They were, Cedric Robinson writes, "Tartar, Greek, Armenian, Russian, Bulgarian, Turkish, Circassian, Slavonic, Cretan, Arab, African and occasionally Chinese". But it was religion, and not slavery, that led to the first emergence of racial thinking. In Spain suspicion of the authenticity of the Christianity professed by the descendants of Jewish and Muslim converts introduced a fantastical discourse about the purity of blood – a discourse that has recognisable links to modern conceptions of race. And it is in Spain that the root of the English term 'race', which first entered the language in the 16th century, is to be found. The Italian term razza, used to describe breeds of dogs and horses, was adapted, as raza, to describe Jews and Muslims as fundamentally separate from Christians.

There was also a gendered dimension to the violence and appropriation that enabled the development of European colonialism, and then, later, capitalism. That violence included the witch-hunt – the public torture and execution of many thousands of women across Europe from the 15th through to the 18th century. As Silvia

Federici has shown, the witch-hunt was not only used to police the bounds of authorised religion. It was also an organised attack on the autonomy of women that functioned to subordinate women to a new and patriarchal form of society in which the commons were steadily appropriated by elites.

1492

In 1324, when Musa Keita I, Emperor of the Mali Empire, made his famous pilgrimage to Mecca, news of his fabulous wealth in gold and slaves arrived in Europe – an altogether poorer part of the world. The Catalan Atlas, drawn and written in Majorca in around 1375, was, for some time, the best map of the known world available in Europe. In this map, painted onto vellum leaves with lapis lazuli, silver and gold, Keita I appears, in regal dress, with an inscription that notes the source of his wealth: "This king is the richest and noblest of all these lands due to the abundance of gold that is extracted from his lands."

In the European myth of Prester John, which reaches back to at least the 12th century, the fabulously wealthy Christian King was first believed to be in Persia, and then India. After Keita I made his pilgrimage to Mecca, Prester John's imagined location shifted to Ethiopia. Portuguese traders began looking to Africa as a source of wealth. In 1419, the Portuguese crown claimed Madeira, an uninhabited archipelago in the North Atlantic. In 1444, Portuguese traders arrived at the coast of Senegal, began to purchase slaves and built a settlement on Gorée Island. They went on to build stone fortresses, feitorias – from which the English word factory is derived – along the Northern part of the Western coast of

Africa. The feitorias were used as nodes in a set of trade networks that included gold, ivory and enslaved people.

Sidney Mintz tells us that sugar cane was first domesticated in New Guinea around 8,000 BC. Two thousand years later it was carried to India where the army led by Alexander the Great encountered it. By 500 AD, sugar was being produced near Baghdad, where it was known as 'the Indian luxury'. It arrived – along with rice, wheat, cotton and citrus fruits – in Southern Europe with the Arab invasion of Spain in 711. In the Crusader states set up in the Levant after the conquest of Jerusalem in 1099, sugar cane was grown with a mixture of free and forced labour. "Europeans", Mintz concludes, "became producers of sugar as a result of the Crusades."

In 1452, sugarcane plantations, based on the model of the Crusader plantations but worked by African slaves, were set up in Madeira. In the same year Pope Nicholas V issued a bull, Dum Diversas (Until Different) authorising the Portuguese King to "invade, search out, capture, and subjugate the Saracens and pagans . . . as well as their kingdoms, duchies, counties, principalities, and other property . . . and to reduce their persons to perpetual servitude".

Constantinople fell to the Ottoman armies, led by Mehmed the Conqueror in 1453. Athens fell in 1458. The Ottoman Empire was building an army, and a navy, that would become the most powerful in Europe. At the same time the European elites depended on Muslim traders to access spices from Asia. The desire to capture this lucrative trade, and to undermine part of the basis for Muslim prosperity, lead to increased interest in the possibility of a sea route to Asia.

Christopher Columbus, an ambitious trader born in Genoa, sought to stake a personal claim on this possibility. He had read Marco Polo's account of his travels to the East and concluded that he could sail west and reach Japan. Columbus was married to the daughter of a sugar plantation owner on Porto Santo, an island close to Madeira. In 1482, he had sailed with the fleet that built São Jorge da Mina, a Portuguese feitoria on the coast of what is now Ghana.

On 3 August 1492, Columbus set sail from the port of Palos, in Andalusia in Spain. The opening line of his diary records that: "In the same month in which their Majesties issued the edict that all Jews should be driven out of the kingdom and its territories, in the same month they gave me the order to undertake with sufficient men my expedition of discovery to the Indies." His diary reveals an obsessive interest in gold.

Columbus, expecting to arrive in Japan, arrived at the Bahamas on 12 October. His diary entry for that day observed that the inhabitants of the islands "should be good servants". He left a group of men on an island he named Hispaniola (now Haiti and the Dominican Republic), with the instruction to search for gold. In May the following year, Pope Alexander VI issued a bull granting Ferdinand and Isabella the right to conquest, to "full and free power, authority, and jurisdiction of every kind", in the New World. This affirmation of a right to conquest and expropriation drew on a set of ideas – like Terra Nullius – first developed during the Crusades.

For Enrique Dussel: "Modernity dawned in 1492 and with it the myth of a special kind of sacrificial violence which eventually eclipsed whatever was non-European." For Walter Mignolo, 1492 is the moment at which "there is a bifurcation of history". For Sylvia Wynter: "(T)he 1492 event would set in motion the bringing together of separated branches of our human species within the framework of a single history that we all now live, and while it led to incredible techno-scientific and other such dazzling achievements, as well as to the material well-being of one restricted portion of humanity, it also led to the systemic large-scale degradation and devalorization, even the extinction, of a large majority of the peoples of the earth."

When Columbus returned to the Caribbean in 1495, his journey funded, in part, by wealth expropriated from Jews and Muslims in Spain, he took sugarcane with him. But his first priority was still the pursuit of gold. The men that he had left on Hispaniola on his first voyage had been killed after abusing the people on the island. Columbus undertook the search for gold with the kind of monomania that Herman Melville would later write into the character of Captain Ahab. It took the form of a genocidal holocaust. He also enslaved hundreds of people – some of whom were sold in the slave markets of the Mediterranean. The pursuit of gold and silver, via appropriation and – as Andrés Reséndez's new book shows – enslavement, would soon wreak genocidal devastation across the Caribbean, and then in large parts of what is now Latin America.

In the Caribbean it would be the plantation, and in particular the production of sugar, that would continue to result, on a staggering international scale, in the ruination of some and the wealth of others. Various dates, ranging from 1501 to 1505 are given for the arrival of the first enslaved Africans in Hispaniola – usually thought to have come from Spain. Bartolome de Las Casas, whose father had sailed with Columbus in 1492, became a key figure in the shift to an economy based on African slavery. Las Casas sailed to Hispaniola in 1502 and, in 1510, was the first priest to be ordained in the New World. He was appalled at the genocidal treatment of the Taíno people and believed that, because there had been no previous Christian presence in the Americas, they could not be legitimately considered as 'enemies of Christ'. In 1514, he began to oppose the enslavement and murder of the Taíno people, initially recommending that Africans replace them as slaves. In 1517, the first major shipment of enslaved Africans arrived. At this time enslaved people in the Caribbean included Muslims, Jews, indigenous people and Africans and slavery was not assumed to be marked on the visible appearance of the body.

In 1522, the first recorded slave revolt was organised in Hispaniola. Enslaved Africans, in some accounts reported to have been Wolof Muslims, rebelled on a sugar plantation belonging to Diego Columbus, Christopher's son. Some of them were able to escape into the mountains and form Maroon communities with Taíno people. At the same time there was acute political conflict in Europe. A massive peasant rebellion raged across German-speaking Europe in 1524 and 1525. The Twelve Articles adopted by the insurgent peasants in Memmingen on 20 March 1525 demanded freedom, democracy and access to the commons. The rebellion was put down with mass slaughter – estimates of the dead range from one to three hundred thousand.

Conflict in Europe would continue for more than three centuries as the enclosure and expropriation of land, and then proletarianisation, gathered pace giving rise to various kinds of heretical ideas and then, beginning in the eighteenth century – with the French Revolution of 1789, the uprisings across Europe in 1848 and the Paris Commune of 1871 being the key events – modern forms of secular radicalism. Popular rebellion would consistently push the ruling class in Europe to seek to contain the social and political crisis at home with wealth wrung from expropriation and slave labour in the colonies, new markets attained abroad and land expropriated for European settlement.

The Portuguese established their first settlement in Brazil – which they initially called 'The Land of the True Cross' – in 1532. In 1537, Pope Paul III declared the doctrine of Anima Nullius, empty souls, with regard to the people of the Americas. It was closely articulated to the doctrine of Terra Nullius. The justification for domination, exploitation and extermination remained theological. As in the Caribbean, the first people to be enslaved were mostly indigenous.

In 1545, the Spanish started mining silver, with slave labour, at Zacatecas, in what is now Mexico, and Potosí, in what is now Bolivia. The mines produced fabulous wealth for the Spanish crown – in a single year more than two hundred tons of silver were shipped to Spain from Potosí. It rapidly became one of the most populous cities in the world and is frequently mentioned in Adam Smith's Wealth of Nations. The wealth went to Spain from where it was disbursed, often via debt repayments, throughout Europe, and on to the Ottoman Empire and China. The influx of silver resulted in a massive increase in currency, began to displace the once more or less absolute feudal link between land and wealth and played a central role in enabling the development of international trade – particularly between Europe and China, and, to lesser extent, India. It has been argued that silver from the Americas was a central factor in the steady strengthening of Christian Europe against the Islamic world. It also seriously weakened the gold markets in West Africa. Eduardo Galeano famously wrote: "You could build a silver bridge from Potosí to Madrid from what was mined here – and one back with the bones of those that died taking it out".

The first ships bringing slaves from Africa to Brazil, most of whom would be set to labour on sugar plantations, arrived in 1570. Four or five million people would follow in the next three hundred years. In 1609, the Moriscos, the descendants of Muslims converts to Christianity, were expelled from Spain.

The English in the New World

In 1606, King James I of England and Scotland, who had been an enthusiastic witch-hunter in Scotland in his youth, made a major bid for influence in the New World. He issued a charter that enabled the appropriation of land in Virginia. It declared that the new colony was intended to "bring the Infidels and Savages, living in those parts, to human Civility".

The Virginia Company, formed in the same year, pooled capital, much of it accrued from the enclosure of common lands in England. The model of joint stock investment had been pioneered in the 1580s under the previous monarch, Elizabeth. Jerry Brotton's new book shows that, facing hostility from Catholic Europe, Elizabeth had looked to Iran, Turkey and Morocco for trade and, in the case of Morocco, military support. This was financed by The Turkey Company, set up and sustained with investments from a variety of shareholders. In 1607, the Virginia plantation was founded in Jamestown – around the same time as the Plantation of Ulster in Ireland (described by the King as 'a civilizing enterprise'). Race, as it was understood at the time, was ascribed to the Irish – who were being forced off their land and replaced with English and Scottish settlers – as well as the inhabitants of what, for Europeans, was the New World.

By 1609, the Virginia plantation founded in Jamestown was in crisis. The colonialists were so short of food that, in the winter to come, they would resort to cannibalism. On 2 June 1609, a fleet of nine ships set sail from Plymouth to relieve the colony in Jamestown, Virginia. The fleet carrying supplies and six hundred passengers – ranging from aristocrats to people dispossessed by the enclosure of common lands in England – was led by the Sea Venture.

On 25 July 1609, the Sea Venture ran into a terrible storm. After days of trying to seal leaks and pump water out of the ship, the sailors lost heart, defied their captain and his gentlemen, opened the rum and prepared to meet their deaths. But, on 28 July, the ship ran aground on the island of Bermuda with no loss of life.

The island offered an abundance of food and temperate weather and many of the sailors, dispossessed at home and exploited at sea, wanted to remain in this new luxury. In nine months the sailors organised five conspiracies against their superiors. But, with execution as a disciplinary mechanism, order prevailed. Two new ships were built and, in May 1610, the bulk of the party proceeded on to Jamestown. Later that year William Shakespeare, who had invested his own wealth in the Virginia Company, used accounts of the wreck of the Sea Venture to begin to write The Tempest. The play was first performed before King James I in London on 1 November 1611.

In The Merchant of Venice, written somewhere between 1596 and 1599, the quality of the mercy extended to the character of Shylock is, at best, strained. Prester John's name makes a passing appearance in Much Ado About Nothing. Othello, written in 1603, is the last in a set of three plays to feature Muslims as characters. In the estimation of some scholars it was inspired, in part, by the six-month visit to Elizabeth's court by the Moroccan ambassador, Abd al-Wahid bin Masoud bin Muhammad al-Annuri, in 1600. But it is The Tempest that is often taken as an allegory for the colonial situation. Sylvia Wynter reads the play as a record of the moment at which the ascription of race – of "humans who can be not quite human" – began to shift from the theological to the secular, mapped onto what Frederick Douglass first called 'the colour line' in 1881.

The Tempest

The Tempest is set on an island after a shipwreck. Miranda, daughter of Prospero, the Duke of Milan, is chaste, obedient, tender, graceful, beautiful, and, as her name suggests, a 'wonder'. At one point, she, a woman defined against a raced other, is described as a 'Goddess'. Miranda's radiance is explicitly set against the shadow of Caliban – her father's slave. His name is often assumed to be an anagram of the Spanish word canibal, from which the English cannibal is derived. Columbus had introduced the term canibal into Spanish. He used it to refer to the people he encountered in the Caribbean.

In the play, Caliban is presented as 'hag-born', 'filth', and, although 'honoured with/A human shape', a 'monster' described as both 'scurvy' and 'abominable'. Prospero tells Caliban that:

> . . . I pitied thee,
> Took pains to make thee speak, taught thee each hour
> One thing or other: when thou didst not, savage,
> Know thine own meaning, but wouldst gabble like
> A thing most brutish, I endow'd thy purposes
> With words that made them known.

Prospero is convinced that Caliban has his daughter in his sights and is bent on rape. In 1952, Frantz Fanon would observe that: "Prospero adopts an attitude toward Caliban that the Americans in the south know only too well."

Miranda's radiance is also implicitly set against the absence of any women from among Caliban's people. We hear white representations of his mother, 'the foul witch', the 'damn'd witch Sycorax' from Algiers who has the power to control the moon. In 1960, George Lamming observed that Sycorax "arouses [Prospero] to rage that is almost insane". Caliban asserts his claim to the land in her name: "This island's mine, by Sycorax my mother". But Sycorax herself, Sycorax as a person, is always absent. Miranda is the only woman on the island.

Wynter argues that when the modern world was formed in the Caribbean: "the only women were white and Western . . . you had true women on one side, the women of the settler population, and on the other you had Indianwomen and Negrowomen".

Land. Labour. Language. Rape. The gendering of race and the racialization of gender. Much of the basic grammar of the colonial condition is here. Much of it remains intensely contemporary. It's no wonder that Caribbean writers, of various kinds, including Frantz Fanon, Aimé Césaire, George Lamming, Sylvia Wynter, Paget Henry, Neil Roberts and, most recently, Safiya Sinclair, have returned to The Tempest again and again.

Césaire initially set out to translate the play into French but found himself rewriting it: "When the work was done, I realized there was not much Shakespeare left". In Césaire's reworking of the play, first published as A Tempest in 1969, immediately after the global tumult of 1968, the black woman remains absent. But Caliban's first word is 'Uhuru!', he demands to be called 'X' and prefers death to "humiliation and injustice". Caliban's final remarks to Prospero come straight out of the black power moment of the time.

The European Ideology

As English power grew in the New World, fuelled at first by sugar plantations worked by African slaves in Barbados and Jamaica, the theological justification for racism was steadily replaced with secular ideologies. The claims of Christendom began to give way to the claims of Europe. The insistence on a unique descent from Ancient Greece and Rome became central to the ideology that presented Europe as set apart from the rest of the world – as the original home of truth, justice and beauty. In time it would become an explicitly racial claim ascribing classical Greek civilization to 'Aryan' migration from the North. It was what Romila Thapar has called "historical memory without history".

All kinds of chauvinisms and lines of exclusion and domination marked the ancient Mediterranean. But the distinctions between people imagined as civilized and barbarian, between colonisers and the colonised and masters and slaves, were not tied to modern ideas of race. There were, in modern terms, white slaves and black intellectuals, artists, merchants and religious, military and political leaders.

The English word slave – and its equivalents in other Germanic as well as Romance languages – comes from the word Slav, a term used to describe people in what is now Eastern Europe. It first appeared in Byzantine Greek in around 800. It would be more than 800 years before slavery was tied to a recognisably modern idea of race, to ideas of whiteness and blackness.

Neither the Greek nor the Roman empires imagined themselves as European projects. Europe was the name of a place, not a political project or a certain kind of people. Ancient Greece and Rome were far more entangled with parts of Africa, Asia and the Middle East than parts of Europe. This entanglement generated the primary spatial basis for the networks through which ideas and technologies were exchanged. It would have been more likely for a person from what is now Egypt, Turkey or Syria to have standing in these empires than someone from what is now, say, Norway or Poland. From Alexander the Great to Julian, the last pagan Emperor of Rome, the drive to conquer was never articulated to anything like the modern conception of race. Culture, not biology, was the primary mark of exclusion and that exclusion was not always absolute – empire offered possibilities for various kinds of routes into inclusion.

The great thinkers of Greek antiquity were well aware that their civilisation came after that of Mesopotamia and Egypt. There were well-established links to Phoenicia and Egypt. Figures like Herodotus and Pythagoras were thought to have visited Egypt. Aristotle's teacher, Eudoxos of Knidos, had studied in Egypt. Aristotle was, Martin Bernal writes, "clearly fascinated with the country". In the 330s, when Alexander III of Macedon, who had been tutored by Aristotle as a boy, conquered Egypt and Persia, and made forays into India, there was a marked escalation in Greek interest in these civilizations – and exchange of various kinds. And the Roman Empire was far from being an isolated or singular civilizational achievement. There were, at the same time, significant empires like the Sasanians in Persia, the Yuezhi (later Kushan) in China and the Guptas in India.

The Many-Headed Hydra

Ideology did not produce consent. The English ruling class encountered resistance at every turn. Enclosure, appropriation and forced labour of various kinds, including, of course, enslavement, were all challenged. In Europe, Africa and the New World, as well as at sea, there was constant mutiny, revolt, heresy and escape. As Peter Linebaugh and Marcus Rediker explain in The Many Headed Hydra, for more than two hundred years, beginning with the start of the English colonial expansion in the early seventeenth century, the new ruling class imagined itself – in terms of ancient Greek mythology – as Hercules subduing the monstrous many-headed hydra – "a symbol of disorder and resistance". Women denounced as witches, vagabonds, heretics, pirates, commoners and colonised people defending their land and autonomy, Maroons and rebellious slaves all appeared as a monstrous hydra that "justified the violence of the ruling classes, helping them to build a new order of conquest and expropriation, of gallows and executioners, of plantations, ships, and factories".

As the plantation system was developed in the New World, forced labour was imported, initially from Europe, and then from Africa. In the 1620s, the majority of the forced labour in Virginia was English. By some accounts what Robinson called 'the terrible culture of race' was not yet sutured to the body. Theodore W. Allen argues: "When the first Africans arrived in Virginia in 1619, there were no 'white' people there; nor, according to the colonial records, would there be for another sixty years." He writes that he could find "no instance of the official use of the word 'white' as a token of social status" prior to its appearance in a 1691 law: "Others living in the colony at that time were English; they had been English when they left England, and naturally they and their Virginia-born children were English, they were not 'white.'"

In 1649, there were still radical struggles in England, largely commoners resisting enclosure in the name of heresy. Their opposition to domination and dispossession at home sometimes extended to a universal commitment to equality and freedom. In 1649, Gerrard Winstanley, a leading thinker in The Diggers, a movement that occupied land, wrote that: "As divers members of our human bodies make but one body perfect; so every particular man is but a member or branch of mankind". Later that year he asserted that the Earth was a common treasury "for whole mankind in all his branches, without respect of persons."

The Radical Enlightenment

In Amsterdam, Baruch Spinoza developed the most significant radical thought in European philosophy. Jonathan Israel calls it the philosophical basis for the radical Enlightenment – a democratic challenge to religious and political authoritarianism committed to universal equality. For Israel: "(T)here is no scope for ignoring the universal conviction during the revolutionary age, beginning in the early 1790s, that it was philosophy that has demolished the ancient régime, and in particular the ideas, beliefs, and loyalties on which it rested, and that it had accomplished this feat long before the first shots were fired at the Bastille."

Spinoza influenced Jean-Jacques Rousseau and Denis Diderot and, via the people he came to influence, the French Revolution. Later on, he was Karl Marx's favourite philosopher. Fanon had a copy of Spinoza's Ethics on his shelf when he died in Tunis in 1961.

Spinoza's ancestors had fled the Portuguese Inquisition in 1536. His father, Miguel, was a merchant. There is some evidence that Miguel's business included trading in sugar from the Spanish plantations in the Canary Islands. Some of Spinoza's contemporaries were linked to the sugar plantations in Brazil. In a letter written in July 1664, Spinoza described a waking hallucination: "One morning, as the sky was already growing light, I woke from a very deep dream to find that the images which had come to me in my dream remained before my eyes as vividly as if the things had been true – especially the image of a certain black, scabby Brazilian whom I had never seen before. For the most part this image disappeared when, to divert myself with something else, I fixed my eyes on a book or some other object. But as soon as I turned my eyes back away from such an object without fixing my eyes attentively on anything, the same image of the same Black man appeared to me with the same vividness, alternately, until it gradually disappeared from my visual field."

However we interpret Spinoza's philosophy, and his own political intentions, there is no doubt that, again and again, the dominant currents of radical politics developed in Europe during the Enlightenment did not take a genuinely universal form. On the contrary Europe was falsely conflated with the universal with the result that most people were expelled from the count of the human and, when revolution came to America and France, the rights of man.

Spinoza's hallucination allowed the African enslaved in Brazil, a category of person that does emerge explicitly in the philosopher's books, to (momentarily) emerge from the unconscious. This episode evokes Dussel's idea of the 'underside of modernity' – but without Dussel's explicit conclusion that "truth and justice" require the retrieval of "the non-hegemonic, dominated, silenced, and forgotten counter-discourse, namely, that of the constitutive alterity or underside of modernity itself."

Liberalism

In Virginia, elite anxieties around popular solidarities were escalating. Linebaugh and Rediker give a good account of this. In 1662, servants and slaves, European and African, gathered, on a number of occasions, to hear heretical preaching. Two years later, an act was passed in Maryland to prevent English women marrying African men. In 1667, the colonial elites in Jamestown expressed their concern that European servants would "fly forth and joyne" with African slaves in Maroon communities.

In Allen's estimation the ascription of race as we still know it today – "a monstrous social mutation" – emerged as an attempt to contain popular solidarities that became a real threat to colonial authority during the uprising, known as Bacon's Rebellion, in 1667. It began as a demand for more aggression against indigenous people by freed men and small farmers seeking land, but turned into a struggle against forced labour by slaves and indentured workers. On 19 September 1676, the rebels, white and black, burnt Jamestown to the ground.

When the King's representative had to negotiate against armed servants and slaves, European and African, he sought to divide them by offering the Europeans relative privilege. William Petty's early attempt to offer scientific legitimation to the ascription of race – which would increasingly be imagined as a matter of the body – appeared in the same year. Philosophical legitimation, with thinkers like John Locke and David Hume doing the initial work, would follow.

Linebaugh and Rediker explain that: "The self-conscious segmentation of the plantation proletariat became even more evident in legislation of 1682 providing that 'all servants not being Christians, being imported into this country by shipping' (i.e., Africans) should be slaves for life, while those who came by land (Native Americans) [who at the time constituted the majority of the people who had been enslaved] should be servants for twelve years. European servants continued to serve only four to five years. Virginia's big planters began to substitute African slaves for European indentured servants." Europeans were given "supervisory and policing positions". Allen argues "in Virginia, any persons of discernible non-European ancestry after Bacon's Rebellion were denied a role in the social control buffer group, the bulk of which was made up of laboring-class 'whites'. In the Anglo-Caribbean, by contrast, under a similar English ruling elite, 'mulattos' were included in the social control stratum and were promoted into middle-class status." The die was cast. More than twelve million Africans would be enslaved and shipped to the New World. Modernity would not just be profoundly raced – it would be fundamentally raced.

Allen's conclusion repeats that of the historian (and first prime minister of Trinidad and Tobago) Eric Williams who, in his 1944 book Capitalism and Slavery, concluded that "Slavery was not born of racism; rather, racism was the consequence of [New World] slavery." Whiteness and blackness were developed in the Caribbean and the Americas. As W. E. B. Du Bois wrote in 1920: "The discovery of personal whiteness among the world's peoples is a very modern thing . . .The ancient world would have laughed at such a distinction".

On 11 September 1683, the armies of the Ottoman Empire were defeated at the gates of Vienna. Although Greece was still under Ottoman rule the idea of Europe as a Christian project, long secured on the Iberian Peninsular to the South, was now also secured from the East. The enclosure of common lands, in the Old World and the New, along with the mines and then the plantations in the New World became the economic foundation of the modern world. The new systems of domination – rooted in racism – were increasingly legitimated via secular philosophy and science.

John Locke is often described as the 'father of liberalism' and the 'philosophical founder of America'. His Two Treatise of Government, written in 1689, is a foundational liberal text. Locke was directly involved in slavery and colonialism. He took the view that lands governed in common – be they in Europe or the Americas – rather than as private property mediated by money, were 'waste' – 'waste' that could and should be redeemed by expropriation. He offered explicit legitimation for the repression of the Irish and the dispossession of Native Americans – who he described as "not . . . joined with the rest of mankind". For Locke, liberal equality could apply only to "creatures of the same species and rank".

Domenico Losurdo, the Italian philosopher and historian, has shown that liberalism was initially grounded in the idea of sacred and profane space – with rights only applying in the former. But as English power expanded into the New World the idea of a sacred realm of rights increasingly came to be marked out by race rather than solely by geography. Whereas England was once the sacred space of freedom and, say, the Caribbean, a profane space where a different set of social arrangements applied, white bodies came to be sacred and therefore sacrosanct, and black bodies profane, and therefore disposable, wherever they were.

In 1684, Francois Bernier, the French physician who had been the personal doctor for the son of the Mughal emperor Shah Jahan, published A New Division of the Earth – often said to be the first attempt to classify humans into races based on physical appearance. Science, like religion before, had become an ideological tool legitimating an often-murderous drive for wealth and power.

In Observations on the Feeling of the Beautiful and the Sublime, published in 1764, Immanuel Kant, making reference to Hume, declared that: "The Negroes of Africa have by nature no feeling that rises above the trifling". His Über die verschiedenen Rassen der Menschen (On the Different Races of Man), published in 1795, is often taken as a key text in the development of modern theories of race. After Kant figures like G.W.F. Hegel, Arthur Schopenhauer and Charles Darwin would continue this ideological work.

Capitalism

Commerce was becoming central to new forms of accumulation. Ian Baucom argues that Liverpool, was "among the shipping, trading, and financial entrepôts" that "ushered into existence our long contemporaneity".

Liverpool, he concludes, was "a capital of the long twentieth century". When a new Exchange was built in Liverpool in 1754, it was circled with series of friezes containing representations of African heads. The following year it was attacked by sailors – who struck for better wages under red flags and were met with cannons taken from the ships in the docks. The sailors' riot, which did not extend its concern to the enslaved, was put down with lethal violence.

In 1781, a syndicate of Liverpool investors bought a slave ship, the Zong, that had been captured from the Dutch. The syndicate included William Gregson, a former mayor of Liverpool, who had invested in fifty prior slaving voyages. The ship was moored off Accra and the deal included the two hundred and forty four enslaved people already on board. Luke Collingwood, a surgeon, captained the Zong. Doctors were often used to select people for purchase as slaves, and to determine the value of slaves. On 18 August, it set sail for Jamaica. A navigational bungle resulted in the ship passing Jamaica. The ship's supply of water was running low. The insurance that had been taken out on the enslaved people would not pay out if they died on shore or from natural causes at sea.

It would, however, pay for cargo that had to be jettisoned to save the ship. A decision was taken to count the enslaved people as cargo – as commodities. Beginning on 1 November, one hundred and twenty three people were thrown overboard. The last ten chose to jump over board rather than allow themselves to be thrown off the ship. On 22 December, the Zong arrived in Jamaica with 208 enslaved people on board. They were soon sold. Compensation was sought from the insurers in London. They refused to pay and legal proceedings began in March 1783. They jury found that the enslaved people were cargo, that they were commodities.

For Baucom, in this moment the value of human beings was not tied to their "embodied, material existence" but to "an utterly dematerialized, utterly speculative, utterly transactable, enforceable, and recuperable pecuniary value". This, he argues, was the moment, the event, following which finance capital, an abstraction, began its domination over the material realm of the human.

Marx was right to observe that "capital comes dripping from head to foot, from every pore, with blood and dirt". The history of the emergence of capital in Europe was brutal. In his study of the public performance of capital punishment in London as a disciplinary tool, Linebaugh called the 18th century English state a thanatocracy – a government of death. But as European radicalism, a project with global ambitions, developed it would, despite Marx's later writings, the work of Rosa Luxemburg and Vladimir Lenin on imperialism, and Antonio Gramsci's innovations, including his essay on the Southern question, often tend to fetishise the factory, initially in Europe, as the central site of domination and resistance. One result of this is that, Robinson argues, when "Black radicalism became manifest within Western society as well as other junctures between European and African peoples ... Western radicalism was no more receptive to it than were the apologists of power".

A strikingly different analysis was developed in what Robinson called the black radical tradition – "an accretion, over generations, of collective intelligence gathered from struggle" that "cements pain to purpose, experience to expectation, consciousness to collective action". In Black Reconstruction, published in 1935, Du Bois wrote that: "Black labor became the foundation stone not only of the Southern social structure, but of Northern manufacture and commerce, of the English factory system, of European commerce, of buying and selling on a world-wide scale; new cities were built on the results of black labor, and a new labor problem, involving all white labor, arose in both Europe and America." Three years later, in A History of Negro Revolt, C.L.R. James arrived at a similar conclusion: "slavery seemed the very basis of American capitalism."

In Robinson's analysis the black radical tradition did not only understand capitalism as originating from slavery, rather than transcending it. He argues that it also took black life and struggle seriously and that its leading intellectuals – he examines Du Bois, James and Richard Wright in some detail – were "troubled by the casual application of preformed [Marxist] categories to Black social movements".

Revolution and Racist Rationality

The French Revolution of 1789 is often taken as a key event in the emancipatory trajectory of modernity. But as Losurdo has noted: "Slavery is not something that persisted despite the success of the three liberal revolutions [in Holland, England and the United States]. On the contrary, it experienced its maximum development following that success." As always there was also an ideological dimension to this.

V.Y. Mudimbe shows that during the eighteenth century Enlightenment social scientists actively worked to legitimate the ascription of race: "The key is the idea of History with a capital H, which first incorporates St. Augustine's notion of providentia and later on expresses itself in the evidence of Social Darwinism. Evolution, conquest, and difference become signs of a theological, biological, and anthropological destiny, and assign to things and beings both their natural slots and social mission. Theorists of capitalism, such as Benjamin Kidd and Karl Pearson in England, Paul Leroy-Beaulieu in France, Friedrich Naumann and Friedrich von Bernhard in Germany, as well as philosophers, comment upon two main and complementary paradigms. These are the inherent superiority of the white race, and, as already made explicit in Hegel's Philosophy of Right, the necessity for European economies and structures to expand to "virgin areas" of the world."

The most significant breach against despotism legitimated and organised in the name of race was the revolution, largely fought by Africans from what is now Northern Angola and the Southern Congo, that resulted in the proclamation of the independent black republic of Haiti on the first day of 1804. Toussaint Louverture, the first leader of the rebellion, drew on an explicit commitment to a universal humanism to denounce slavery.

Colonialism defined race as permanent biological destiny. The revolutionaries in Haiti defined it politically. Polish and German mercenaries who had gone over to the side of the slave armies were granted citizenship, as black subjects, in a free and independent Haiti.

But liberal thought sustained its investment in the ascription of race as a fundamental feature of modernity. John Stuart Mill's On Liberty, published in 1859, is, arguably, the second great text of the liberal tradition. Mill, who spent most of his adult life, working for British colonialism, began his argument on the question of liberty by asserting, in passing, that: "Despotism is a legitimate mode of government in dealing with barbarians."

Mill was no outlier. The accumulation of capital, enabled by racism, meant that certain forms of cultural, academic and scientific power could be concentrated in Western Europe and North America. These forms of power were frequently used to reinscribe the fundamental ideology of modernity. Robinson, writing in 1983 about the silencing of the Haitian Revolution in Europe concluded that: "it was their ideologues, their intellectuals, their academies that succeeded in the larger suppression". Almost twenty years later he argued that the "corrupt association between American science and race" in the 19th century was sustained by the dismissal and hounding of "those critics whom they could not summarily dispatch."

In The North African Syndrome, an essay first published in 1952, Fanon gave a characteristically acute account of how academic authority, in this case scientific authority, was enmeshed with racism. He wrote that in the French medical establishment: "(T)he attitude of medical personnel is very often an *a priori* attitude. The North African does not come with a substratum common to his race, but on a foundation built by the European. In other words, the North African, spontaneously, by the very fact of appearing in the scene, enters into a pre-existing framework. In other words, medical science in colonial France allowed *a priori* ontological assumptions to prevent it from making rational sense of experience."

This deception of reason, this collapse into what Lewis Gordon calls "racist rationality", results in racist societies producing forms of knowledge that, while authorised as the most fully formed instances of reason at work, are fundamentally irrational.

A Counter-Humanism?

We are all, in the sense derived from Walter Benjamin, formed from the catastrophe of history. Some of us have come out of that catastrophe with property, wealth, education, social standing and access to the agora. Others are impoverished, socially-scorned and governed with welfare, incarceration and violence. Some of us are valued. Some of us are disposable.

On 9 August 2014, Michael Brown, an unarmed black man, was shot dead by a white police officer in Ferguson, Missouri. The movement that grew out of the rebellion that followed inaugurated a new sequence in the struggle against racism in the United States. As with previous sequences in that struggle it quickly acquired an international dimension, including here in South Africa. One aspect of this international moment has been an urgent confrontation with the reality that what Césaire called 'abstract equality' does not, on its own, mark an end to the racialization of life.

In the United States, and elsewhere, there is a sense that history is as present as it is past. Just over a decade ago, Baucom observed that "what-has-been is, cannot be undone, cannot cease to alter all the future-presents that flow out of it. Time does not pass or progress, it accumulates". It is the sense that time accumulates into the present that has often led to the invocation of William Faulkner's famous line from Requiem for a Nun in discussions about race: "The past is never dead. It's not even past."

The past does not merely haunt or shape the present via the enduring power of deep and impersonal structural forces. Across Europe, and in settler societies like Australia, Brazil and the United States, racism is an increasingly explicit and menacing presence at the centre of political and social life. White revanchism has rallied, often under demagogic leadership, to secure the racial order that emerged from the event of 1492. It has already resulted in Brexit in England, the impeachment of an elected President in Brazil and the election of a figure as grotesque as Trump in the United States.

We will not be able to transcend the epoch that began in 1492 without a politics that can confront and defeat this revanchism. And we will not have transcended this epoch until "things, in the most materialistic meaning of the word" are, as Fanon insists, "restored to their proper places". But the catastrophe from which we are all derived is not solely a matter of material dispossession and accumulation. As Michael Monahan argues, in conversation with Wynter, "the history of colonialism is also the history of the emergence of the idea of Europe and of Europeans, and . . . it is such ideas and cultural practices that inevitably shape our consciousness, conditioning what counts as normal and, ultimately, as rational".

For Wynter, the accumulation of crisis cannot be posed as a serious question, understood or resolved "within the conceptual framework of our present order of knowledge". The production, authorisation and dissemination of knowledge are not, at all, the sole province of the university. But in South Africa it is in the university where the breach in the established order that followed the murder of Michael Brown has acquired most intensity.

Wynter's insights speak to the university as a site of contestation with particular acuity. It is, she notes, "the 'best and brightest' products of our present system of education; of its highest levels of learning" that sustain the accumulation of crisis. She argues, following Fanon, that the university will only be able to work against the order from which it emerges, and is sustained, when its intellectuals are able to shift the ground of reason into the terrain of the liminal, into new forms of mutuality with people defined as "pariahs outside the sanctified order". She insists that the imperative to mutuality requires that reason, as it is developed in the academy, be enmeshed with "the degradation of the jobless, of the incarcerated, the homeless, the archipelago of the underdeveloped, the expendable throwaways".

What Wynter calls "a counter-humanism made" – and here she borrows from Césaire – "to the measure of the world" requires that we "for the first time, experience ourselves, not only as we do now, as this or that genre of the human, but also as human". This is a matter of praxis. It requires, "the transformation of our original dominant/subordinate social structure and its attendant perceptual and cognitive matrices into new ones founded on reciprocal relations". This mutuality can also be the basis for the kind of emancipatory praxis – the constitution of new forms of organisation and popular democratic power – that was often developed out of the encounter between dissidents in our universities and wider society in the '70s and '80s.

About the author

Richard Pithouse is a Research Associate at the Wits Institute for Social & Economic Research at the University of the Witwatersrand, the editor of New Frame and the Coordinator of the Johannesburg office of the Tricontinental: Institute for Social Research.

www.ingramcontent.com/pod-product-compliance
Lightning Source LLC
Chambersburg PA
CBHW070818280326
41934CB00012B/3221